I0559946

My Amazing Toddler
Behavioral Series

I Count To Three.

I Am
BRAVE!

An Affirmation-Themed Toddler
Book About Being Brave (Ages 2-4)

By

Suzanne T. Christian

TWO**RAVENS**
B O O K S

Two Little Ravens
CHILDREN'S NON-FICTION BOOKS

Paperback Edition: 9781964202716
Hardcover Edition: 9781964202723
Digital Edition: 9781964202730

Published in the United States by Two Ravens Books LLC,
254 Chapman Rd, Ste 209, Newark DE 19702

'Expand the mind, free the imagination, one title at a time.'
www.tworavensbooks.com

Welcome to
"I Count To Three.
I Am Brave!"

This is a happy book of simple-to-comprehend affirmations created for toddlers learning to confront new and occasionally frightening things.

As you read these playful pages with your child, they'll learn that being brave doesn't mean you're not scared, it means you try anyway, with a sprinkle of humor and a lot of heart.

Each page features bright and engaging real-life situations your toddler can relate to, such as visiting the doctor or meeting new friends. With the positive affirmation "I am brave!" and the calming repetition, your child will learn to build courage and resilience, one moment at a time.

Bring this book into your child's daily life to help them develop emotionally, laugh with all their heart, and say with confidence, "I can do it!" Buckle up for a thrilling ride of bravery, imagination, and overwhelming feelings reduced, affirmation by affirmation.

Suzanne T. Christian

Being brave means trying, even when I feel scared.

I try one bite,
even broccoli trees.
Crunch! I am brave!

When I see a bug on the wall, I smile and say, **"Hi, little friend!"**

At daycare, I hug goodbye.
I know my grown-up
always comes back.

When I feel shy,
I whisper,
"I can do it."
I am brave!

I use my big smile and say
"Hi!" to new friends.

I count to three,
then I slide down,
wheee!

One step, two steps,
I climb higher each
time. I am brave!

Oops, I fell. I giggle, then stand up again!

I sit still while the doctor listens to my heart. **Ba-dum, ba-dum!**

I jump in the
pool with a
splash and a
giggle.
I am brave!

Haircuts tickle my ears,
I laugh, not cry!

When I hear thunder,
I say "Boom!" right back.

I open wide so the dentist can count my teeth. I am brave!

I roar louder than
the vacuum cleaner!
I am not afraid!

When I'm nervous,
I take deep breaths, ahhh.
I feel better! I am brave!

My nightlight shines and chases scary shadows away! I am brave!

When it's dark,
my teddy hugs me tight.

I Count To Three.

I Am

BRAVE!

The End!

My Amazing Toddler Behavioral Series

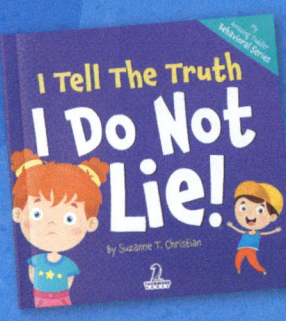

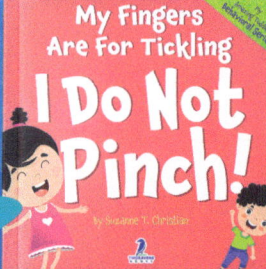

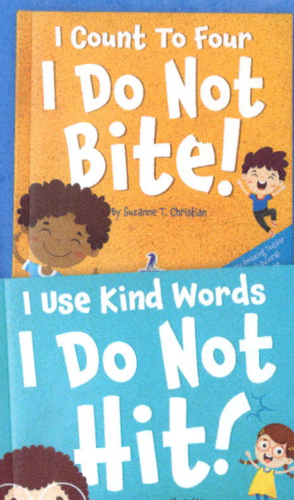

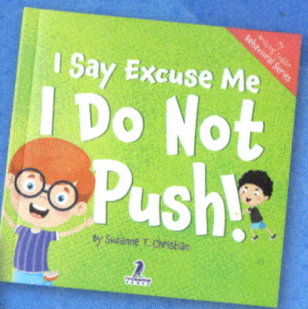

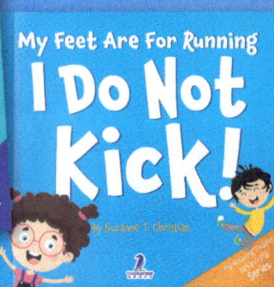

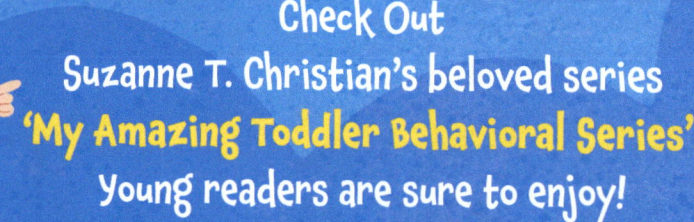

Check Out
Suzanne T. Christian's beloved series
'My Amazing Toddler Behavioral Series'.
Young readers are sure to enjoy!

Two Little Ravens
CHILDREN'S NON-FICTION BOOKS

Dear Amazing Reader,

Thank you for diving into **I Count To Three. I Am Brave!** with me. If this book touched your heart or made a difference for a young reader, I'd be grateful if you could share your thoughts in a review. Your feedback inspires my future work and helps others discover the magic within these pages.

I'd love to hear from you directly if you have suggestions or ideas for improving the book. Please feel free to reach out to me at **suzanne.christian@tworavensbooks.com.** Your voice counts, and I cherish it deeply.

With heartfelt gratitude,